Praying the Psalms

by
John Goldingay
Principal, St. John's College, Nottingham

gb GROVE BOOKS LIMITED
Bramcote   Nottingham   NG9 3DS

CONTENTS

FOREWORD

In Grove Spirituality Booklet 41 on *Evangelical Spirituality* I trailed my coat regarding evangelical spirituality's assumptions about prayer. In adhering to a tradition of prayer which has developed during the past century or so within evangelical piety, it has ignored the dynamic of the life of prayer implied by the Psalms, scripture's own manual of praise and prayer. One or two members of the Grove Spirituality Group trod on this coat, and the present booklet is the result. Its framework goes back to a set of Quiet Day talks at Lincoln Theological College but it also reflects material I have used in the Old Testament course and in the Spirituality course at St John's College, Nottingham, and I am glad to express my indebtedness to students and colleagues whose presence, comments, and questions have so contributed to what appears here.

Where not otherwise indicated, biblical quotations are from the New Revised Standard Version.

I have treated some of the issues which appear below in *Poetry and Wisdom: Eight Bible Studies for Students and Young Adult Groups* (Bible Society, Swindon, 1987).

First Impression February 1993

ISSN 0262-799X

ISBN 1 85174 232 8

INTRODUCTION

I recently marked an ordinand's essay on the Psalms in which he began by relating what a new experience it has been at college to use the Psalms systematically in worship and to discover the way they could draw him into praise and prayer that expressed and developed his own life with God. In none of the three parish churches to which he had belonged had he experienced the use of the Psalms in Sunday services. He then reflected that admittedly, had he belonged to a church where they were used in the traditional way, ironically this would perhaps have put him off them rather than winning him.

The Psalms are dying in the Church of England. It once expected its worship to include an average of six Psalms every day. My own recent experience of Sunday services in a variety of parish churches parallels that of the ordinand I have quoted. The most common deviation from the ASB's rubrics is the omission even of the reduced psalmody the ASB prescribes. A feature of *Patterns for Worship*[1] is to widen the scope of what is allowed within statutory services and thus make possible a reining-in of unauthorized deviation; the Psalms thus need only 'normally' be used. I fear the effect is to canonize the idea that they are dispensable.

Of course the problem cannot be solved by legislation. If people are not convinced that the Psalms express worship and prayer which they can and need to offer, forcing them to use them is no more useful than it is practicable. My concern here, then, is to point to something of what that ordinand had discovered through beginning to use this indispensable resource of praise and prayer.

[1] A Report by the Liturgical Commission of the General Synod of the Church of England, GS 898 (Church House Publishing, London, 1989); see page vii.

1. OUR WORD TO GOD, GOD'S WORD TO US

Sometimes the beginning of a scriptural text gives us important pointers regarding how to read it. The books of the prophets commonly open by providing us with information about their origin in a human author (though one who brings God's revelation) speaking to a particular audience in a particular historical context, as if to say 'You will only understand the messages that follow against this concrete historical context'; something similar is true of the Epistles. Luke begins his Gospel by telling us his aim in writing it, and John does something similar at the end of his.

In a parallel manner, Psalm 1 introduces the Psalter as a whole by encouraging us to meditate on God's Torah or Teaching. Where is this Teaching to be found? Perhaps Psalm 1 refers to *the* Torah, the 'Law', and implies that only those who live by this Torah can read and use the Psalms aright—which would certainly fit what the prophets have to say about the relationship between worship and life. Perhaps it hints at the idea that the Psalms themselves have become a resource for teaching as well as a hymnbook—God's word to us as well as ours to God. The rest of scripture speaks to us, but the Psalms speak for us, Athanasius declared. But by being in scripture they also speak to us. The Psalms which spoke to God now speak for God, reveal God's ways, and reveal to us the kind of prayer and praise God encourages. The Psalter has become Torah: it is even divided into five books like the Pentateuch, with doxologies like the Gloria at the end of each (Psalms 41; 72; 89; 106; with Psalm 150 as a doxology to the whole).

Psalm 1 invites us to be open to God's word. Psalm 150 closes off the Psalter as a whole with a summons to praise which is unique because it gives no reasons for the praise—the reasons are contained in its 149 predecessors. At the end the Psalter can content itself with 'lyrical self-abandonment'.[1] As the Psalter unfolds, the way from the obedience of Psalm 1 to the praise of Psalm 150 goes via candour about suffering (which faces the questions left unfaced by the assurances of Psalm 1) and gratitude about hope; it is a way which has Psalm 73 as a halfway staging post as it journeys between these two poles.

---

[1] W. Brueggemann, 'Bounded by Obedience and Praise' in the *Journal for the Study of the OT* 50 (1991) p.67.

2. THE PSALMS AS WORSHIP

Individual psalms also commonly begin with some introduction, though the details of the meaning of these introductions are obscure. In general, however, what they do make clear is that the Psalms have a background in the context of worship (for instance, indicating how or when to sing them). This may seem an obvious and uncontroversial point, but it has not always been so. Until a century ago interpreters of the Psalms took the same approach to their interpretation as they would take to the prophets, asking when the text was written and by whom. They varied widely in their results, however, and it was only through the work of the pioneer form critic Hermann Gunkel that the penny dropped that the reason people disagreed about the origin of the Psalms was that the Psalms conceal more than they reveal regarding their historical background. Historical interpretation works against their grain, and in fact fails to work.

As a form critic Gunkel put study of the Psalms on the track of two questions which are more illuminating than 'When was each of the Psalms written?' The first is 'What are the recurrent ways of speaking to God which feature in the Psalms—what different types of Psalm are there, and what are their internal dynamics?' The second is 'What are the recurrent social contexts of these ways of speaking to God—the kind of recurrent situations in which people write such Psalms and use them?' The answer to the first question is that the Psalms reflect three recurrent ways of speaking to God. Psalms of praise and worship rejoice in who God is and what God has done to redeem. Psalms of lament and prayer emerge from contexts when God does not seem to be acting in a redeeming way for individual or people. Psalms of thanksgiving or testimony confess what God has done for individual or community in response to such prayer. Gunkel also drew attention to other types of Psalm such as those bringing God's word to the king, but we will focus on the first three types because of their significance for our concern with praying the Psalms.

Gunkel's answers to that first question were of long-term significance for our use of the Psalms. His answer to the second question was wide of the mark, though instructively so. Gunkel could tell that the content and the introductions to the Psalms pointed to Israel's worship in the temple as the social context in which psalmody flourished. He could also tell that the Psalms were the expression of real spirituality. But Gunkel was a good Protestant who knew that the worship of the temple was ritualistic, cultic, quasi-catholic, and spiritually dead, so how could its psalmody be the expression of a true relationship with God? He resolved this dilemma by concluding that most actual examples of psalmody in the Old Testament come from the post-exilic period and reflect its individual piety (because that is the only form of true piety), even though they reflect the forms of the pre-exilic temple.[1]

The breakthrough in perceiving the now-obvious fallacy in Gunkel's reasoning came in the work of a pupil of his, the Norwegian scholar Sigmund Mowinckel. He did his key work in the 1920s, even though his comprehensive work on the Psalms was published in English only in the

[1] See his introduction to *The Psalms* (Fortress, Philadelphia, 1967) pp.26-29.

1960s.[1] He pointed out how significant is public worship for any religion, Christian or not. For Protestants as much as for Catholics public worship is of vital importance as the occasion when the community meets together and meets with God, and when its fellowship and its relationship with God is encouraged to grow towards maturity. For Protestants as well as for Catholics, too, the acts and forms of that worship take regular, socially-established forms, whether or not these are formally enshrined in a prayer-book. This being so, there is no longer any obstacle to our understanding the Psalms in the obvious way, as the hymnbook of Israelite worship.

[1] *The Psalms in Israel's Worship* (Blackwell, Oxford, 1962/Abingdon, Nashville, 1963).

3. THE PSALMS AS WORLD-CREATING PRAISE

In looking at the Psalms' actual worship, their praise, we may begin with the single piece of scripture that recurs most often in the worship of the Church of England (the Lord's Prayer alone excepted), Psalm 95, the Venite. 'Come, let us cry out to Yahweh, let us shout to the Rock who saves us. Let us come before his face with thanksgiving, let us shout to him in psalms.' Its beginning is thus noisier than our translations indicate, and it contains no word for 'joy'—that is smuggled in to make the Psalm sound more religious than it naturally does. The Venite begins with an invitation to a fervent, exuberant, out-loud confession that God is God.

The invitation is renewed later in the Psalm, in very different terms. 'Come, let us bow down prostrate, let us kneel before Yahweh our maker.' Again the translations make the Psalm more Anglican than it is. It contains no word for 'worship'. The verbs are all body-words. Having opened like a charismatic praise meeting the psalm continues like a moslem observance of Ramadan.

In the Psalms we relate to God as whole people, and moderation is not among the Psalms' vices or virtues. They deal in extremes, and invite us to join them there. They presuppose that relating to God is not a matter of slouching or sitting but of leaping and bowing. When we come before God, we do not abandon the self-expression and body-language, the enthusiasm or gloom, of the pub or the sports field. Worship is a matter of shouting and weeping.

There are two sets of reasons why shouting and bowing down are appropriate responses to God. On one hand, it is because 'the LORD is a great God and a great King above all gods.' That is a more polemical statement than it sounds. 'The LORD' here stands for the name of Israel's own God, Yahweh (the Jerusalem Bible is the one version not to obscure this fact throughout the Old Testament). Yahweh is the only being who has divine or kingly power.

Now the Israelites were surrounded by people who acknowledged other gods and other kings, people who said that Baal was a great god or who acknowledged Shalmanezer as the great king. In that context, to affirm 'Yahweh is a great God and a great king' was a bold confession, an exercise in what a sociologist might call world-creating.[1] To declare 'Yahweh is a great God' is a profoundly political statement; worship is not an escape from life in the world.

Indeed, when we worship we thus take the world into the presence of God with us, so that we can name God's name over it. We look the world in the face and look in the face the questions that trouble us—and the developments that excite us—and declare over them 'Yahweh is God,' 'Jesus is Lord.' In the power of that confession we then take the world and its questions more seriously, because it carries with it the promise that they can be faced. In worship we affirm how we believe the world to be, despite what

[1] See W. Brueggemann, *Israel's Praise* (Fortress, Philadelphia, 1988).

7

we see. We do not create this new world—it already exists as the real world, the world of God. In the light of affirming that it is the real world, we then live in the world in that conviction.

We cry out our praise to God, then, because God is creator and sovereign. We then bow down in prostration because this God is our God and we are this God's people or flock—the almighty creator, the great king, is our maker, our shepherd. I think I would have expected the Psalm's logic to work the other way round—to offer God's almightiness as grounds for reverent submission and God's shepherdly caring as grounds for enthusiastic thanksgiving. The Psalm's own logic is less predictable but more profound. We glory in the fact that God is the creator but then kneel in reverence in the light of the fact that this creator and sovereign has condescended to be our maker and shepherd.

God's involvement with the world and with us as creator is actually a theme that runs through the Psalter. Psalm 104 illustrates that involvement with the world particularly well. It affirms the wonder of creation, the generosity of God that creation reflects, and the lordship of its God even over the realm of darkness. It offers a variety of models for God's relationship with nature—starting it off, being the very locus of the energy and system of nature, being personally involved in the present, acting in the manner of the 'God of the gaps' bringing about calamities and disasters. Elsewhere the Psalms affirm the security of a world in which the powers of darkness cannot reassert themselves (Psalm 93). They wonder at the way the cosmos declares God's glory and at the way the mighty creator is involved with mere human beings (Psalms 19 and 8). They testify that the God who is the creator is thus the God of everyday life and of my everyday experience and need. In the Psalms God is giver, healer, and deliverer more than lawgiver and judge. Yahweh is not just the God of the past (history) and the God of the future (eschatology) but also the God of the present, of worship and everyday life.

---

[1] See W. Brueggemann, *Israel's Praise* (Fortress, Philadelphia, 1988).

4. PRAISE AND COMMITMENT

After the enthusiastic but reverent worship of the first part of the Venite comes a stanza with a quite different tone. The first part is a hymn of praise, comprised of an invitation to worship and the reasons for worship, the two features of a hymn of praise in the Psalter. The Jubilate, Psalm 100, has the same two features, and even the same double structure— invitation, reasons, renewed invitation, further reasons. It also has much of the same imagery.

But then the Venite and the Jubilate diverge, because the latter has nothing corresponding to the last part of the Venite. Psalm 95 stops being a hymn and becomes a kind of prophecy. So far it has been doing what the Psalms normally do, speaking Godwards. The last stanza of Psalm 95 reverses this movement. Instead of addressing God, we find ourselves being addressed in God's name: 'If only you would listen to him now!' For seven verses we have been making God listen to our voices, telling God how enthusiastic we are and how willing to prostrate ourselves. Then God speaks back.

I wonder how the Venite came to have this form? I like to romance that verses 1-7 once existed on their own as a perfectly good hymn of praise, used year-in year-out in the temple for generations. Then on some specific festival occasion, perhaps, some priest or prophet was given a word of response to the people's worship, which then became attached to it. The divine response says, 'O shut up for a minute and listen, will you? You're all enthusiasm and prostration. That talk about God being your king and shepherd: is it mere talk?' A more respectable, less romantic view of the origin of Psalm 95, I should add, is that the Psalm was written that way because it linked with the kind of occasion when Israel recalled its deliverance from Egypt and its entering into covenant relations with God at Sinai. The beauty of the Psalm is that it combines the worship and the commitment which are both parts of a proper response to the God of redemption.

The exodus generation shouted aloud when they saw God act, but their submission to God did not carry over from words to life. The psalm does not question that people meant every hallelujah and every genuflexion, but it does ask whether what they meant in worship was matched by what they did outside of worship. 'Where do you place your trust? Who directs your path? I know what your words and hearts say about that, but what does your life say? If your life belies your words and feelings, you forfeit your share in God's rest.' Our worship has professed to make a link with life. Is the link real?

It is suspicious that we now shorten the Venite so as to omit the stanza which makes it distinctive, the words with which God responds to our worship, and replace them with words which refer to God judging the world instead (a verse from the end of Psalm 96, with which the Venite closes in its ASB form).

Psalm 95's challenge to commitment links with one of the features of the Psalms which often offends modern Christian readers (not ancient

9

Christian readers, as far as I know). When things go wrong in our lives or we lose touch with God, we instinctively blame ourselves. The point is classically expressed in the question on the church poster, 'If God seems far away, guess who has moved?' The Psalms view that as an open question. Sometimes they acknowledge human failure as the reason for God's moving away, and pray 'out of the depths' of human sin and chastisement (Psalm 130; cf 51). On other occasions they affirm that they have kept their commitment in the way Psalm 95 challenged them to (see e.g. Psalm 44.17-18). That is part of the basis for their appeal to God to act. In the same way, at the end of Psalm 139, after calling on God to act in judgment on the wicked who oppose God's purpose (God's enemies, not ours!), we ask God to test our hearts and see if there is any wickedness in us. We are not saying 'O dear, perhaps I should not have prayed that prayer'. We are saying 'Look into my heart to make sure I really meant my opposition to people who oppose you and am not secretly in sympathy with them'. Like Job, in affirming their commitment the psalmists are not claiming to be sinless. They are making a claim about the fundamental commitment of their lives. We have to be able to make that claim and survive the challenge of the last part of Psalm 95 if we are to be able to praise God authentically.

5. THE LINK BETWEEN LIFE AND LITURGY

The insights of Gunkel and Mowinckel which encourage us to see the Psalms as literary texts and as liturgical texts could have a down side. In our own hymnbooks and worship books there are prayers and praises (not least metrical versions of the Psalms) which look as if they were written to order rather than because someone had met with God. Perhaps there are Psalms which had an origin of that kind, when an Asaphite had to produce a new Psalm for Passover because the choir was tired of the old ones. Gunkel himself is not alone, however, in recognizing that characteristically the Psalms reflect real experience of God on the Psalmists' part. The praise and prayer of the Psalms belong first in life and only derivatively in worship.

The point can be illustrated from the occurrences of Psalms and psalm-like praise and prayer elsewhere in the Old Testament. If the people Israel in the strict sense comes into being in Exodus, then its prayer life begins with an agonized helpless cry arising from a labour camp. As such prayer belongs first in life and not in liturgy, so does the praise which recognizes that God has overheard the people's cry even though that cry may not have been uttered with God in mind—it was just a helpless cry (see Exodus 2; 15). Later Hannah does pray and praise at the shrine, but she prays out of the reality of life experience, in the grief, hurt, and anger of a woman who cannot have children and is despised for it, and when Yahweh answers her prayer and she has her baby, she praises at the shrine out of that reality too (1 Samuel 1-2).

Job's prayer begins at the shrine but when real life intervenes his prayer continues in the place of affliction itself—not least the presence of his friends. Jonah seeks to escape from the face of God (a phrase which rather implies he was in worship when he received his word from the Lord, as one might anyway expect) but found himself called to prayer on a foundering boat, drawn to praise in the midst of a large fish, and initiating a resentful conversation with God in the streets and outside the walls of a pagan city. Jeremiah, too, finds himself drawn into a prophetic ministry which requires him to declare prophecies that God is not committed to fulfilling, in his case to a people who will not listen to them because they are bent on self-destruction. The combination commits Jeremiah in turn to living between the upper millstone of danger because of the content of his words and the lower millstone of ridicule because of their emptiness, experience is the engine of his prayer life (Jeremiah 11-20).

Praise and prayer belong first in life and derivatively in worship. The same is true of our hymns. Their power and their meaningfulness derive from their having emerged from real people's personal turning to God, with which our experience resonates even though we may not know precisely what their experience was. It is significant that another of the great writers on the Psalms this century, Claus Westermann, came to his study out of the context of the German church struggle of the 1930s. In the preface to his study of The Praise of God in the Psalms he notes how 'in the present transitions and disasters the church has been confronted anew with the question of the praise of God'.[1] There the church praised God as well as prayed 'out of the depths' (Psalm 130). People discovered that there they learned not only how to be steadfast but how to praise.

[1] See *The Praise of God in the Psalms* (Knox, Richmond, 1965/Epworth, London, 1966; expanded edition, *Praise and Lament in the Psalms* [Knox, Atlanta/Clark, Edinburgh, 1981]) p.5.

6. PRAYER WHICH HOLDS TOGETHER TWO SETS OF FACTS

The Psalms deal characteristically in extremes. They deal in extremes of enthusiasm and reverence which indicate that people's praise was not a matter of merely going through the motions. When other agenda dictate the nature of their prayer, they deal in extremes of dark despair, of lonely helplessness, of grief, anger, and hurt in their relationships with other people, in their own spirits, and before God. The Psalms assume that when we talk to God punches do not have to be pulled nor words minced. Infinitives can be split and emotions expressed. There are hardly any feelings of pain, despair, vindictiveness, or let down that fail to be expressed somewhere among these 150 examples of things you can say to God.

One of the most powerful of those 'laments' is Psalm 22, 'My God, my God, why have you forsaken me . . .?' It illustrates many of the characteristics of this way of praying. It naturally begins by calling on God. We may be less comfortable with the protest with which it immediately continues. The protest and expression of hurt is expressed in three directions. It laments what other people have done to us, insofar as that feels to be the problem ('All who see me mock at me . . . Many bulls encircle me . . . A company of evildoers encircles me . . .'). It draws us into acknowledging how we feel in ourselves ('I am a worm and not human . . . I am poured out like water . . .; my mouth is dried up like a potsherd . . .'). But the point of deepest hurt is where the Psalm starts, with what God has done or not done to us ('Why are you so far from helping me, from the words of my groaning? O my God, I cry by day, but you do not answer . . .'). The Psalm invites us into an extraordinary freedom in our speech with God. This is what it can mean to call on God as 'Abba, Father' (the term is not used in the Old Testament, perhaps because it was too cheapened in Israel's culture—as arguably in ours). And its object is not merely to make us feel better by letting it all hang out (though no doubt it does fulfil this therapeutic function). Its object is 'to summon God away from the throne' (God's position in heaven which our worship celebrates) 'back into human life which is so hurtful and raw'; its object is to mobilize God into action.[1]

Psalm 22 also powerfully illustrates another characteristic feature of lament psalms, their recollection of God's deeds in the past and their statement of trust in God in the present. Indeed Psalm 22's own distinctive power derives partly from the way it holds together the truths about God which the psalmist is committed to living by, and the experience of abandonment and loss which he or she currently experiences. (The 'he or she' is worth making explicit, both because the Old Testament explicitly indicates that its poetry, prayer, and praise can very easily be of female authorship—consider Miriam, Deborah, and Hannah to begin with—and because the psalms are in the Psalter to be used by people of either sex.)

The psalm insists on looking in the face the facts about God and the facts about one's current experience. It refuses to let the first subvert an acknowledgment of the second—unlike Job's friends, who (as Robert Davidson put it) rewrite Job's life rather than revise their theology.[2] People involved in pastoral care meet and include people who have not owned their pain or grief because it threatens their faith and worldview.

[1] W. Brueggemann, *Interpretation and Obedience* (Fortress, Minneapolis, 1991).
[2] See *The Courage to Doubt* (London, SCM, 1983) p.178.

Neither does Psalm 22 let the pains of the present permit a denial of the facts about God. People involved in pastoral care also meet much of that in hospitals and funeral parlours—and in themselves. Psalm 22 insists on looking both sets of facts steadily in the face. It alternates a sense of abandonment, insecurity, and isolation with a poignant recollection of what God is, what God has been to Israel, what God has been to the particular individual who prays, and what God is going to be the other side of this calamitous experience. 'The praise has power to transform the pain. But conversely the present pain also keeps the act of praise honest.'[1]

That is not its only function. Psalm 22 is significant in its own right, but it is also significant as the tortured lament which appears on the lips of Jesus, and as one of the New Testament's key texts for an understanding of Jesus. Nor is it only Jesus who prays with the Psalms of lament. Paul uses a lament such as this (actually Psalm 44) to describe his own experience, in Romans 8. A person who feels the need of New Testament warrant for taking up Old Testament spirituality has it! The psalms of lament are there for us to pray. They speak for us.

Psalm 22 illustrates at its most dialectical a regular feature of the psalms of lament: while they arise out of darkness and near hopelessness, in one way or another they reach out in hope as they contemplate past, present, or future. A further feature of the way they reach out in hope is instructive for our own prayer. It is fervent and straight but quite unspecific in precisely how it expects God to act. Psalm 22 simply pleads, 'Do not be far from me . . . Do not be far away . . . Come quickly to my aid . . . Deliver my soul . . . Save me . . .' What prayer asks for is to be heard and delivered. How God effects deliverance is best left unspecified.

---

[1] Brueggemann, *Israel's Praise*, p.139.

7. PRAYER, PAIN, AND ANGER

When Paul uses the Psalms, and when we do so, we are actually showing that we are walking in Jesus's way. 'If we are to mirror God, to be in God's image, to be like God, to invite God to indwell us so that we live Christ's life . . . we have to be willing to enter our individual wounds and through them the wounds of the community'. The Psalms can be one of our means of doing that. 'The importance of our wounds lies in how we choose to relate to them, how we choose to enter and to integrate them into our lives . . . We must never yield to the temptation to engage, in the name of "healing", a new and often more destructive denial and repression such as T. S. Eliot describes: People change and smile, but agony abides'. We must be prepared to sit in the dark. With the laments, we must be prepared to release our tears. 'Tears are a sign that we are struggling with power of one sort or another: the loss of ours, the entering of God's'.[1]

The most extreme example of this inherently extreme way of praying is Psalm 88. Claus Westermann observed that 'there is no petition that did not move at least one step on the road to praise'.[2] Psalm 88 is the nearest to an exception to this rule, for this expression of utter isolation and abandonment, a cry from the realm of death itself, contains no recollection of God's past acts of love and no statements of conviction about how things will again be. 'Your wrath lies heavy upon me . . . You have caused my companions to shun me . . . I am shut in so that I cannot escape . . . Your dread assaults destroy me . . .'. So it goes on, until in due course it simply stops (rather than finishes).

What has gone wrong in the psalmist's life we do not know. We cannot penetrate behind the metaphorical and symbolic descriptions of the experience to the experience itself. But that is just as well. The fact that the experience is described only in metaphorical and symbolic terms makes it more feasible for us to find ourselves in these words. We too know what it is to be overwhelmed, to have things pressing down on us (demands, burdens, guilts, expectations), to feel insecure, threatened, afraid, forgotten, cut off from God, hemmed in, alone. 'Not waving but drowning.'

I say we do, but I must allow for the possibility that not everyone does. In studying the Psalms with people I invite them to decide whether they find Psalm 88 encouraging or discouraging. They vary in their answer. Some find its dark despair and sense of abandonment inappropriate for a Christian. That may indicate that they are unwilling to look despair in the face, or it may indicate that they are people of particular inner resilience or spiritual resources, or people to whom life and God are especially kind, who do not need to identify with Psalm 88.

I still seek to encourage them to enter into it, for the sake of those they may minister to if not for themselves. There are many in the church and in the world who do weep, and many others who need to do so, and when the Psalms of lament are not functioning as our prayer for ourselves they can

---

[1] M. Ross, *Pillars of Flame* (SCM, London [1988]) pp.xvii, xviii, 124.
[2] *Praise and Lament in the Psalms,* p.154.

become our intercession for the church and for the world. They provide us with a way of entering into the experience of people in need and standing in their place in prayer.

Not that intercession is quite absent from the Psalms. In effect Psalm 72 is an intercession for the king. It suggests God's vision for government—in monarchic terms, though its vision is not difficult to translate into democratic terms—holding together fairness, prosperity, prayer, witness, fame, and victory. It is a telling fact that the prophets' own key terms, judgment, justice, salvation, peace, and blessing all appear here.

The Psalms which pray for vengeance also become our intercession as we pray them on behalf of people who need to express these feelings but are not able to do so (or perhaps who properly pray for their oppressors' forgiveness as we properly pray for their overturning). What are we to say, then, of liturgical reform 'which deprives Christian prayer of the so-called cursing psalms, the instrument by which the poor and the oppressed denounce their historical ills, asking God to do justice by abstaining from doing justice themselves? These are psalms which, while calling on God to establish divine justice, sanction the principle of non-violence, pledging the one who prays not to yield to the temptation to render evil for evil'.[1]

I find that the anger of the Psalms arouses similar mixed reactions to those which apply to the Psalms' hopelessness, but I find that the people who are most offended by it are people whom I suspect to be fooling themselves about their own anger, perhaps repressing it in a very British way. Walter Brueggemann has observed that the real problem lies not in the anger in the Psalms but in the anger in us, and comments on how attuned the Psalter thus is to what goes on among us: there is 'an acute correspondence between what is *written there* and what is *practiced here*'. It offers us the opportunity to face our anger, to express it in words rather than in actions, and thus to own it before God and yield it to the wisdom of the God who also knows anger and gives it expression in the pursuit of justice in history. When we have gone through that process, and only then, 'can our rage and indignation be *yielded* to the mercy of God'.[2] If the death of Christ was God's act of judgment on human sin, it constituted a positive answer to the psalms' prayers for vengeance.[3]

---

[1] E. Bianchi, 'Contemporary challenges to prayer' in *Asking and Thanking* (*Concilium* 1990/3, ed. C. Duquoc and C. Florestan) pp.55-56.
[2] *Praying the Psalms* (St. Mary's Press, Winona, MN, 1982) pp.68, 79.
[3] See D. Bonhoeffer, *The Psalms* (SLG, Oxford, 1982) pp.21-23.

8. PRAYER AND HELPLESSNESS

So in their despair and their anger the Psalms reflect not the shallowness of Old Testament spirituality but the depth of its grasp of what a relationship with God makes possible. The darkest of the Psalms are some of God's most reassuring invitations to us.

Oftentimes we may be faced in our lives and in our prayers with the agony of the silence and the inactivity of God, and may be tempted to wonder whether the actual silence reflects a metaphysical silence, a silence that indicates that there is no-one there, no-one to whom we pray, no-one to speak. In that context, the first words of Psalm 88 take on new significance, given the cries of rejection which they introduce. There is a breathtaking illogic about its conventional opening 'O LORD, God of my salvation . . .' How can you say 'My God' to someone who you believe has turned the other way and stuffed their hands over their ears? The variety in the Psalms is such that sufferers in all sorts of circumstances may be able to find themselves somewhere in them.

Whether in our pain and hurt we triumph, or trust, or cope, or struggle, or despair, there is a Psalm we can use, one which begins where we are. Psalm 88 is in some ways the most precious of them because it is the most wretched and comfortless. A person who has lost all trust, hope, and faith may be able to begin their praying here. Even such a person then finds that in articulating prayer at all they have uttered the words 'O LORD my God.' They are not merely articulating their suffering, letting it all hang out, giving expression to it rather than bottling it up. They are doing these things, but *to* somebody, someone who is there. They have not been drawn out of despair, but they have been drawn into that argument between hope and despair which is needed if they are to face both sets of facts and be true to their experience and true to the God they know. There is no overt step toward praise in Psalm 88, but there is an implicit statement of faith which catches you out when it requires you to utter it.

Psalm 88 is dominated by death. Death is a prominent feature of the Psalter: the possibility of death, the threat of death, the inevitability of death, deliverance from death, the death of someone near you. Perhaps this is another reason why we cannot cope with the Psalms. Death is perceived as not merely the event which finally terminates human life when (if you are fortunate) you have had your three score years and ten. The Psalms have a slightly Johannine view of life and death: life worth living is full life, a life that is truly alive, and when such fullness of life is taken away from us by illness, danger, fear, loneliness, oppression, or depression, it is as if death reaches out into life and takes possession of us even in the midst of life. It is partly for this reason that the Psalms talk about death so much. 'You have put me in the depths of the Pit, in the regions dark and deep . . . Is your steadfast love declared in the grave, or your faithfulness in Abaddon?'

The Psalms talk as if death is the end. Christians may be inclined to find that assumption difficult to relate to, though it has several significances for us even this side of Christ's resurrection. Assuming that death is the end makes people take this life with the seriousness it deserves. It encourages us to live by reality and by evidence—for before Christ's resurrection there was no evidence that human beings would have resurrection life. It reflects the conviction that no-one else is Lord of that realm. It reflects the fact that to someone who feels cut off from God it seems as if death must be the end. It reflects the fact that death is indeed the end if people are cut off from God.

Death is the realm in which praise and prayer are neither uttered nor heard. Yet these very psalms show that it is out of death (out of the prospect of death, out of the death of someone near me, out of some experience of living death) that actually prayer arises at its most powerful. And because such prayers are heard, this mercifully disproves the lament they express, that prayer has no place in the realm of death. The very fact that a person is praying in such a place is one of God's wonders, and the next of God's wonders is that God hears that cry out of the place of darkness.

There is a page or two in an old book on Prayer by Otto Hallesby to which I find myself coming back when I feel that in some way I have reached a cul de sac in prayer, when I do not know how to pray and feel spiritually dry and thus helpless. 'As far as I can see,' Hallesby says, 'prayer has been ordained only for the helpless. It is the last resort of the helpless . . . We try everything before we finally resort to prayer . . . Prayer and helplessness are inseparable.' Only the person who is helpless can truly pray. If I feel sinful or abandoned, cold or depressed, doubting or dishonest, the feeling of helplessness this awareness induces is not my barrier but my way into prayer. 'Prayer therefore simply consists in telling God day by day in what ways we feel that we are helpless.'[1] The Psalms encourage this view.

[1] *Prayer* (IVF, London, 1948), 11, 17.

9. THE PSALMS IN PERSONAL MINISTRY

Ideally, we are not left alone to come to terms with this helplessness. The dynamic of a prayer such as Psalm 22 presupposes that the transition from abandoned lament to anticipated thanksgiving is made possible by the ministry of someone who speaks a word from God to us.

Even if my fantasy regarding the origin of Psalm 95 is indeed mere romance, the Old Testament provides us with substantial evidence that prophets did function within Israel's worship (see especially Chronicles). When people had brought their need before God, someone brought God's word of response to them, and that made possible this transition from lament to praise. The story of Jehoshaphat threatened by invasion provides a spectacular example (see 2 Chronicles 20). The Psalms themselves also provide examples of how a word from God makes possible this transition from plea to praise (see e.g. Psalms 12 and 60). In most cases in the Psalter, however, the actual word from God is not included. Of course one can never prescribe the nature of God's answer to prayer, and this is perhaps one reason for leaving empty the 'space' where one seeks for God's word. Jeremiah's experience shows how the response to a lament may be other than one hopes (see Jeremiah 14-15; also Hosea 6.1-6). God is free to respond in the way God wishes; we can prescribe a way for us to pray, but not a way for God to answer. 'God does speak, but he . . . almost never repeats himself.'[1]

I used to fret at the fact that I could not imagine how Christian worship could ever incorporate the outpouring of the laments in which individuals bring their pains to God, as they need to do; Walter Brueggemann notes how the censoring of their note from Christian worship in favour of a predominant note of praise encourages a triumphalist theology of glory and fails to witness to a theology of the cross.[2] Israel's own practice likely points us to the resolution of this dilemma. Individuals gave voice to such laments in a context that was more like that of a fellowship or prayer group than that of temple worship. The latter may be the natural and effective context for a festival of praise, the former that for prayer for healing and deliverance.[3]

The lament Psalms also have a place in the ministry of individual to individual. The story of Hannah in 1 Samuel 1 again provides an illustration. She comes to pour out her heart to God in her grief, anger, pain, and helplessness, praying the way the Psalms of lament do. With tragicomedy Eli initially misreads the situation and upbraids her for coming near the temple in a drunken state (compare Acts 2); the celebration of the festival no doubt gave him every reason for suspicion. In due course, however, he gets his pastoral act together and brings God's word of reassurance and promise to her, in the way the Psalms presuppose, and after this Hannah can return home with her spirit restored, as the lament Psalms again presuppose happens when a person has had God answer their prayer.

[1] J. B. Metz, in J. B. Metz and K. Rahner, *The Courage to Pray* (Burns and Oates, London, 1980) p.25.
[2] *Interpretation and Obedience* p.194.
[3] See P. D. Miller, *Interpreting the Psalms* (Fortress, Philadelphia, 1986) pp.5-7.

Donald Capps has thus written on the use of the the lament Psalms in grief counselling. The Psalms give people the means of expressing the pain they need to express—but to God. We help them do that, then listen to God for them. As a theological college tutor I used to have a certain amount of experience of people coming to share their pain and hurt (I'm now an authority figure so they go to someone else!). Having stumbled across this feature of the Psalms of lament I found myself encouraging people to use the lament Psalms to express their pain to God when they had explored it with me. Sometimes this was a matter of inviting them to say a particular Psalm which said what they needed to say, sometimes a matter of me saying such a Psalm for them (for saying it themselves could still be too much), sometimes a matter of me turning what they had been telling me into a lament-type prayer on their behalf. My task then was to change positions and listen to God on their behalf (which I found a tricky exercise because it demands a significant move if one has truly been standing in their place), so that one could utter God's word of reassurance (or otherwise!) to them. I believe scripture provides us with a powerful pattern of ministry here.

Communities, too, need to express their grief. Death and mourning can be corporate realities: at the moment of writing I think of the threatened further death of mining communities in the area where I live, and within the sector of ministry in which I work I think of the threatened further death of theological colleges. The broader death experienced by the church in Britain (the death of its old power and significance) raises similar questions. Awareness of the importance of grieving and of the nature of its stages has become part of the conventional wisdom of pastoral care in the 1990s, but an equivalent awareness of the corporate grief process also needs to develop. The Psalms of lament provide resources for the expression of that corporate grief which can be the beginning of new life.[2]

Nor is it only believers who may find that the Psalms speak to them and for them in this way. In 1945, a nineteen-year-old German soldier called Jürgen Moltmann was taken prisoner by the British and eventually placed in a camp in Sherwood Forest, where the Nottingham YMCA set him going on the theological study which eventually took him to being one of the great twentieth-century theologians. Having lived through the horrors of the Second World War, the collapse of an empire and its institutions, and the guilt and shame of their nation, many German prisoners collapsed inwardly and gave up all hope, some of them dying. 'The same thing almost happened to me,' Moltmann testifies, were it not for a 'rebirth to a new life' which turned Christian faith into reality rather than formality. 'The experience of misery and forsakenness and daily humiliation gradually built up into an experience of God.'

[1] See *Biblical Approaches to Pastoral Counselling* (Westminster, Philadelphia, 1981) pp.59-97.
[2] See G. A. Arbuckle, *Grieving For Change* (Chapman, London, 1991).

'It was the experience of God's presence in the dark night of the soul: "If I make my bed in hell, behold, thou art there." A well-meaning army chaplain had given me a New Testament. I thought it was out of place. I would rather have had something to eat. But then I became fascinated by the Psalms (which were printed in an appendix) and especially by Psalm 39: "I was dumb with silence, I held my peace, even from good; and my sorrow was stirred" (but the German is much stronger—"I have to eat up my grief within myself") . . . Hold thou not thy peace at my tears: for I am a stranger with thee, and a sojourner, as all my fathers were." These psalms gave me the words for my own suffering. They opened my eyes to the God who is with those "that are of a broken heart" '. Later Moltmann adds that he does not so much want to say that this is how he found God, 'but I do know in my heart that it is there that he found me, and that I would otherwise have been lost'.[1] Moltmann's testimony may suggest that the Psalms are also a neglected resource for our ministry to a lost world.

[1] From Moltmann, *Experiences of God* (SCM, London, 1980) pp.6-9.

10. THE PSALMS AS TESTIMONY

There is a third way of speaking to God which we have yet to consider. A psalm of praise like the Venite or the Jubilate acknowledges who God is and how God characteristically behaves in relation to the world and Israel. A lament such as Psalm 22 or 88 agonizes over God's failure to act in those characteristic ways and to be that person. A thanksgiving psalm rejoices over some recent personal experience of the turning of God's face and the answering of prayer.

Laments work by their specificness, their systematic outpouring of the supplicant's experience, albeit described in metaphorical terms. Thanksgivings also work by their specificness, now a systematic testifying to the worshipper's experience of deliverance. Psalm 30 illustrates what is happening when we pray a prayer of this kind. It parallels the Venite and the Jubilate in that it goes through a sequence of movements twice, in verses 1-5 and 6-12, though the paragraphing in the ASB obscures the fact. There are four elements in the sequence.

First, I remember how things once were. 'I said in my prosperity, "I shall never be moved . . ."' The recollection is reminiscent of statements of a right confidence in God such as that in Psalm 62, 'God is my fortress; I shall never be shaken,' but it also reminds one of other statements that reflect more a confidence in oneself. Is the psalmist affirming that past spiritual stance of confidence in God, or recognizing now that it reflected a foolish self-confidence? The statement itself is ambiguous, and ambiguity of this kind is an important positive feature of the Psalms. There is an openness about their language. Often they do not tell us which interpretation of their words is the right one; they test us by leaving it to us to decide what we would mean by their words. The most telling example of this phenomenon is Psalm 139, 'O Lord you have searched me and known me.' Is God's knowledge of us good news or bad news? The translations of Psalm 139 vary fascinatingly over the points at which they understand it one way or the other. The Psalm is systematically ambiguous and puts those who pray it on the spot because they have to decide which way they dare mean it or whether they dare say it.

Second, I remember how things went wrong and how I prayed. 'You hid your face; I was dismayed. To you, O LORD, I cried . . . O LORD, be my helper.' The prayer which is recalled further illustrates the nature of the actual plea in a lament. It is very vague compared with the concrete specificness of the psalm's description of the situation and the need. Our prayers tend to suggest to God policies for implementing: 'Lord make the chancellor see that increasing government spending is better than cutting taxes.' Biblical prayer works by describing before God the plight of the needy and then simply urging God to *do* something about it.

Third, I remember how you responded. 'You have turned my mourning into dancing; you have taken off my sackcloth and clothed me with joy.' Once more prayer is a matter of extremes: either lamentation and sackcloth or dancing and joy. The thanksgiving psalms have a further striking feature. Although we may give this title to them, it has been pointed out that they do not use the verb 'thank' so very often. Indeed, the word in question does not quite mean 'thank', but more 'acknowledge', 'confess', or 'testify', and the Psalms commonly go about confessing what God has done without having to say that this is what they are doing. Indeed, the word can get in the way; to say 'I thank you' puts me in the front of the sentence. To omit it offers God the glory even in the syntax: 'You have drawn me up . . . You have healed me . . . You have restored me to life . . .'

Fourth, I rejoice with a joy that extends to other people and to other times. What God does for me deserves also to glorify God and to upbuild the church. Conversely, what God does for other people deserves to glorify God and to upbuild me. So 'sing praises to the LORD, O you his faithful ones . . .' The Psalms assume that we share our griefs and hurts with each other in prayer—we have noted that people did not necessarily or ideally pray laments on their own. They also assume that we share our joys in Christ with each other. We weep with those who weep, and we rejoice with those who rejoice. As I prove that the apparent world is not the real world, I draw other people into my world-creating experience. Like praise and prayer in general, thanksgiving for what God has done for me begins in life and is initially personal to God and me, but it must become public—become confession or testimony. My confession extends to other times as well as to other people: 'you have turned my mourning into dancing . . . so that my soul may praise you and not be silent. O LORD my God, I will give thanks to you forever.'

11. THE DYNAMIC CYCLE OF PRAISE AND PRAYER

There is a sense in which we are back where we began. We began with hymns such as the Venite, with a life committed to praise because of who God is and because of the mercy which lasts for ever. We crashed from height to depth in the laments which confront a God who seems to be silent for ever. In a thanksgiving we have come out the other side of that experience into a praise which breaks silence, in response to God's having broken it first. The entire sequence of praise, lament, and confession which characterizes the spirituality of the Psalms thus appears within Psalm 30 itself (as it does also in Psalm 22).

There is more than one way to characterize their interrelationship. Claus Westermann continues his observation that 'there is no petition that did not move at least one step on the road to praise' by adding that 'there is no praise that is fully separated from the experience of God's wonderful intervenation in time of need'.[1] He contrasts Egyptian psalms, which praise God only in general terms, not in relation to God actually doing anything, and Babylonian psalms, which praise God only as a lead in to prayer, never for its own sake. In Israel what he calls the 'vital, tension-filled polarity of plea and praise' has its centre in the thanksgiving at which we have just been looking, which looks back to lament and forward to ongoing worship of God.

Walter Brueggemann suggests a different analysis of the interrelationship of these three ways of speaking to God. In *The Message of the Psalms*[2] he points out that the sequence praise, lament, thanksgiving corresponds to three stages by which life and faith develop, orientation, disorientation, and reorientation. Orientation implies knowing who you are, knowing who God is, knowing how life works. Disorientation means having those convictions collapse through some experience of loss (or some unexpected joy!). The temptation then is to seek to find our way back to the old orientation—or to give in to disorientation and yield to agnostic despair. The only truly human way out is forward, into a new orientation which does justice both to what was true about the old and to the experience which has exploded it. It is a renewed orientation which does justice to both sets of facts, to use the language we used earlier. Put in worship terms, the move is one from praise, to lament, to thanksgiving or confession or testimony.

To judge from the Psalms, the move forward to reorientation may come in several ways. In Psalm 30 it apparently comes because God does something. In Psalm 22 there is a sudden change of mood two-thirds of the way through which seems to suggest that God has said something, perhaps via a priest or a prophet, which the psalmist has accepted, and this has changed everything. In Psalm 73, which recalls an experience of almost losing faith, the psalmist somehow sees something, and comes to another of the Psalter's extremes, 'Whom have I in heaven but you? And

[1] *Praise and Lament in the Psalms* p.154.
[2] Augsburg, Minneapolis, 1984.

there is nothing upon earth that I desire other than you . . .' The breathtaking confession is only reached because of the 'Why? Why? Why?' of the bulk of the psalm. It was when an old orientation caved in that something new could be perceived.

These two ways of relating lament, worship, and thanksgiving seem mutually exclusive but they are both plausible. This points us to a more dialectical understanding of the relationship. Praise feeds prayer; prayer feeds praise. The relationship is a circular one in which praise can be a beginning or a climax, thanksgiving a midpoint or an end. It would be better to describe the relationship as spiral, for yesterday's fresh new orientation is today's old inadequate one which has to be allowed to collapse. What the Psalms are portraying is an ongoing pattern of life in the Spirit, one which is neither static nor circular nor linear but spiral. They invite us to live in this dynamic cycle of worship and obedience, lament at the experiences of loss and suffering that we have ourselves and share with the church and with the world, petition to God to turn back and act, confession that this has happened, and renewed commitment to worship and obedience which takes us full circle. To judge from individual Psalms, when we need to we can enter the circle at any point and go round it as far as we wish. We will find ourselves passing places we have been before and saying words we have said before, yet meaning new things by them as we come to them out of new experiences as new people.

I was once in a PCC when it was discussing replacing Morning Prayer by Holy Communion as the church's main Sunday service. I allowed myself the opinion that an advantage of this would be that we would be able to get out of singing the wretched Psalms, which I viewed as the most tedious element in Sunday worship. My vicar withered me with a look across the room in a way he had perfected and barked, 'One day, my boy, you will need the Psalms.' He was right. Twenty-five years later, the Psalms are the framework of my life with God, the part of each day's reading of scripture that is most likely to give me matters to take up with God, most likely to encourage me because in their agony they so often start where I may need to start in prayer, and most likely to challenge me because they move from there into a worship whose conviction and enthusiasm I long to emulate.

I cannot understand how Christians can take a superior stance over against the spirituality of the Jewish Bible. The Psalms make me think not, 'Poor Jews that they have this distant legalistic relationship with God,' but 'I wish I related to God the way these Jews did even before Jesus came.' The Church of England needs to recover them.